# Future Self

## The Time Traveler's Interactive Guide

### Becoming Who You Want to Be

**Future Self From the Mind of Michael Horn**

**Cover Design**
Douglas Harkey

**Editor, Formatting**
Jedi Reach (Jedaiah Ramnarine)

**Future Self**
**First Edition** 11/2/2017
Michael@futureself.global

# Disclaimer

*This book is not intended as, nor a substitute for, professional medical advice, treatment, or care, nor intended to advise or treat any medical, psychological or psychiatric conditions that one may have, suffer from, or for which they may be under the care of a professional.*

# Table of Contents

# How It All Began

In 1972, Michael Horn had an unusual and still inexplicable experience, which gave him advance knowledge of three specific healing technologies, two of which were indeed developed subsequently. In 1985, he suddenly felt prompted to develop the one remaining process himself, to the limit of the technologies available at that time.

Now, utilizing digital technologies not available in 1985, he has taken the remaining technology to the next, near final step, as Future Self - The Time Traveler's Interactive Guide - Becoming Who You Want to Be.

Michael previously personally facilitated this interactive, consciousness enhancing, self-analytical, therapeutic technique, which can also enhance any form of meditation, for film makers, political figures, musicians, etc., is now available to anyone to utilize in the comfort and privacy of their own home.

As you read this book, you will learn how to use your computer, lap top, tablet, cell phone, or camera to help you take control of, and responsibility for, your own life and fulfill your own chosen destiny as your...Future Self.

# Time Travel

It's not surprising that with the ever-increasing stresses, the environmental destruction and geo-political upheaval, time travel is very much on people's minds today and the topic of much science fiction and futuristic media.

Time travel is actually a concept that's fascinated people for a very long…time. The idea of going back to the past, or of visiting the future, holds great interest for us and has given birth to all sorts of fantasies, theories, books and movies, etc.

While we can't yet travel back in time to see what history was really like, each of us already has our own personal history, however long or short it may currently be. We each have our own hopes, dreams, wishes and visions of the kind of future we'd like to have, which have often been mainly limited by our agreeing to the limitations that we've let *others* place upon us.

# Flowments

To travel to the future, we begin where we are, in what's called the present, or the present moment. But the present *doesn't* really exist, as the moment isn't a static place or thing, it's a series of pulses flowing ever-forward, perhaps best described as *flowments*. These flowments are what we ride upon as we traverse time, moving inexorably into the future, becoming our… future selves.

# Mirror, Mirror on the Wall

If we could travel back in time 8,000 years, we'd see the first mirror, the first human invention deliberately intended to give us a reflection of ourselves. While you can watch yourself in the mirror doing various things...the mirror doesn't make, or keep, a recording.

We'd only have to go back about 300 years to see the first photograph from a still camera that captured a moment in history. Then came cameras that could record motion over *time*, and which we've used mainly to entertain, as well as educate, ourselves. As an evolution of the mirror, video and film cameras enabled us to passively observe, more than to really *interact* with, ourselves...until now.

With the technology genie out of the bottle, one might think that the process of attaining *self*-knowledge would be even faster and easier. But despite all the readily available technology and information in this digital age, many people hardly know themselves at all. The rampant selfie epidemic has done little to improve self-understanding, mainly encouraging narcissism and superficiality, bypassing attention on anything substantial, or of more than momentary interest.

Consequently, people often plunge forward into the future haphazardly and without deliberation and conscious choice.

But technology itself isn't to blame; tools can be used for different purposes, both good and bad. When used in an evolutive manner they can enable us to expand our awareness of who we are, tap into our own innate wisdom, clarify our goals and values, and actually help us to achieve them.

The purpose of this book is to illustrate and provide one way that can be done, utilizing what I call the Future Self interactive experience and self-therapeutic technique. You'll learn how to explore the content of your own past, and even use it to create the future *you* prefer, as the person *you* wish to become.

Future Self can help you to develop your self-awareness, tap into your innate wisdom, initiative, imagination, realism and optimism. These qualities are, by and large, atrophying and disappearing among much of the population, as people have become more passive consumers and entertainment seekers, looking to, and exalting, others as their heroes.

Having personally facilitated many Future Self sessions, I initially considered finding someone to create a software program to assist people to do the Future Self process themselves. In fact, years later, some people did do experimental online, software based attempts at creating a limited, interactive program.

But the answer turned out to be even simpler because, with easy access to ever more sophisticated devices with video cameras, anyone can now facilitate their own Future Self experience. This book provides the protocols, or instructions, on how to proceed.

# So, You're Hearing Voices?

First, some information about me, my own original Future Self experience and the educational video process that I subsequently created around it.

In 1972, I was living in a small apartment in Venice, California, having recently survived a stint of homelessness in New York City, where I got by largely by luck, adaptability, and the grace and generosity of other people. That is a story in itself but it will have to wait for another time.

Having effectively begun a completely new life, I was mainly focused on writing songs, playing guitar and performing at various coffeehouses in Santa Monica and Venice. One morning, I was sitting on the mattress on my bedroom floor, waiting for the so-called voice of inspiration, my lined yellow paper tablet in one hand and a pen in the other.

I had the familiar feeling that I was about to come up with a lyric for a song. Some people who are familiar with writing songs, poetry, etc., may experience this as a "voice" speaking, or dictating, the words to them. But instead of anything particularly lyrical or poetic, I heard this, verbatim:

"I am your future self, come to you across a bridge of time, built by you and others like you, that you may know you are an eternal being."

This certainly was not the kind of inspiration I was expecting, but I wrote it down nonetheless.

Writing a song usually involves a kind of flow, often with a rhythmic feeling as the words and ideas take form on the page. But this was different. It was more like something being described to me in an informational way. It was followed by brief descriptions about three different developments in healing technologies that I would supposedly learn about in future times to come. They may not seem so dramatic now, many years later, but certainly at the time these things were completely unknown to me and indeed perhaps they didn't yet exist. I certainly had no conscious knowledge about any of them.

*Briefly, they were...*

## Optimal Frequencies for Health

The first modality dealt with the idea that specific, optimal frequencies of each bodily organ and gland, etc., are associated with, and contribute, to the overall state of health. In the years to come, we would learn how to identify the specific frequencies connected to the different organs and states of health, and then adjust, or tune, ourselves to these frequencies, in order to improve our health. The way to do this would be similar to biofeedback, something that we already had at that time, in 1972.

Of course, some of these technologies may have already existed in various forms *before* I had my experience. There are today different modalities that purport to measure various frequencies in the body, such as machines based on Rife technology, and the equipment developed by Dr. Reinhard Voll, etc. I didn't know anything about any of these technologies at the time, though perhaps I could have picked up some information in an unconscious way.

# Light and Sound

The second future healing modality described a special chamber where the patient would stand while their body, and so-called "energy body", acupuncture meridians, etc., would be scanned, displayed and evaluated for diagnosis by technicians/healers. They would then administer the specific, scientifically determined, corrective sound and/or light frequencies to the bodies, to aid in healing.

We've already seen developments in science and healing pertaining to frequencies, the use of light and sound, etc. There's also a biological technique dating back to around 2000, called optogenetics, which could be a form, or application, of what was described utilizing sound and light directed at body.

# Psycholograms

The third healing modality was called Psycholograms, and described a future time in which people would go to special institutes and make "personality deposits", i.e. they would be interviewed and recorded regarding a very wide range of personal data. This data would be stored in a centralized computer, along with that from all of the other participants.  This presumably would also include similar information about historical and even mythological figures, in order to be available for inclusion in a Psychologram, i.e. a simulated *holographic* interaction.

Each participant would have computer access to the centralized program, whereby their holograms and associated information would also be available to be used by the other participants, something like, but far more advanced than, what are *now* called avatars in video games, etc.

The holograms in the Psychologrems program would be created from the audiovisual record of the actual participants, with the computer generation of the historical and mythological figures. A forerunner to this may be the new technology for motion pictures that allows deceased movie stars to be visually revived/reanimated, i.e. showing them in performances they never gave, strictly recreated from their past audio-visual material.

To have a Psychologrammatic Interaction (PI), the required information would be entered into the personal computer, including who is in the PI, where it is occurring, what the subject, situation or topic of the PI is, how long it should last, etc. Other participants from around the world could be chosen from the data bank.

These could be real people, and/or the aforementioned historical and mythological people, whose holograms would have been created by Psychologrammatologists, from the accumulated data. Even various figures from comic books, movies, etc., might be licensed for inclusion and also be displayed as holograms.

For example, one could choose to create a scenario in which they were traveling on a space ship with Captain Kirk, Joan of Arc, Martin Luther King, Wonder Woman, Albert Einstein, along with someone they've never actually met, living somewhere else in the world, perhaps even Billy Meier, or one of the Plejaren, etc.

The topic or situation would be chosen, such as traveling through time, or dimensions, to visit another world or planetary civilization, even a simulated business meeting, etc. It could also be something far more mundane, such as a probable interaction pertaining to a business situation, cooperative project, etc. The person could choose to either generate *their own* hologram, and observe its interaction with the other holograms, or to participate and interact from a special chair.

The special chair would be equipped with various built-in sensors, to monitor and record the participant's conscious and unconscious *psychological* responses, emotions, etc., hence the term Psychograms. When the PI was over, they could replay it, with (or without) the computerized description and analysis pertaining to the psychological information and insights that could be gained from it, depending on their preference.

This third modality, Psychograms, describes a form of full-blown virtual reality, without any glasses or headset, etc., with the projection of holograms and use of technology to monitor one's own internal reactions, etc., to computer-generated interactions.

It was this element that would, later, give rise to the Future Self video technique. Because you can now do the important part of the process yourself, in the privacy of your own home, the only remaining element would be the interaction with the holograms, which indeed may not be all that far away in the future.

# "Get a Video Camera"

In 1985, while I was doing some errands, I felt an inner prompting to get a video camera. I initially dismissed it because I had no *need* for a video camera. Or so I thought. The impulse reappeared and again I dismissed it. When it occurred for the third time, I decided to...*get a video camera*. I quickly went and purchased a Kyocera from a camera store in Santa Monica, California.

As soon as I got in my car to return home, I had the sense that I was *supposed* to do Future Self sessions, connected to my earlier experiences, in 1972. The process began flooding into my mind. At stoplights and stop signs, I started jotting down notes, specific question, etc. Once I was home, I called a woman I knew, named Susan, and I invited her to come over and do a Future Self session. Of course, she asked me what that was.

I told her to just come with an idea about something that she wanted to do, have, or become, which she hadn't yet accomplished. Oddly, I was enthusiastic to do this process on someone else, before I had done it on myself, which I did later.

Susan's was the first session of many I did, on a wide variety of people. Some later came back to give me video testimonials about having accomplished the very thing they had done their Future Self session about. This included a woman who wanted to, and later did become, a citizen diplomat between the US and what was then called the Soviet Union; a film producer, who came back a year later to show me the film he'd produced, which fulfilled the goal of his Future Self session; and a professional background singer, whose goal was to sing back-up for Michael Jackson, which he did later in Japan, 1987.

# Overview of the Future Self Process

A unique aspect of Future Self is that you will actually interview *yourself.* Using the provided format, you will answer a number of specific *implied* questions, designed to elicit information about yourself, in a wide variety of areas and categories. In this way, you are accessing and depositing, for your own review, information about a wide range of things, both positive and negative, that have been part of creating your life experience up until now.

There are no wrong answers. You are just trying to *see things as they are* and stating information in a neutral manner. When you later assess the information, you will honestly determine those things that are already clear and useful and those which may need more work, further strengthening, etc.

We define success for ourselves. To become truly successful, we must also be very honest with ourselves. True self-esteem isn't something that someone else can give us. It's solely based on our own real accomplishments and recognition of them. The positive self-esteem that results from seeing what we are capable of can open up tremendous, positive energy to fuel our striving towards our goals, with a confidence born of the knowledge and recognition of real accomplishment.

Because a core purpose of Future Self is to regain complete authority over one's own life, the information you are remembering, and revealing is intended solely for your own review and evaluation. You're not accountable to anyone but *yourself* in this process. Of course, should *you* wish to share this content with someone, such as a therapist, counselor, close family member, etc., it's up to you.

Because each person is an individual with often vastly different life experience, the volume and nature of information provided in response to the questions can vary greatly. There is no set, mandatory time frame for doing the complete process. It needn't be rushed, or done all at once, etc.

You are about to create, to re-create yourself and your life as you want it to be. You will define your goals, the things you most want to accomplish, outline the steps you need to take, and strive towards your goals, step-by-step.

*Now, let's begin the process by...*

## Preparing for the Interview

To proceed, you will need at least one of the following:

*Smart Phone, Laptop, PC/Desktop, Tablet, Video Camera*

**Optional**:

*A second recording device*
*(such as one of the above)*
*A TV*
*A notepad (or just use one on your device)*

The Interview helps to bring to the foreground of our awareness *many* things that are not always in the forefront of our consciousness in our daily lives, but which still may be affecting us in different ways.

Think of the Interview as a *download,* with you effectively searching – not the internet – but your own *memory* from your personal, built-in hard drive and downloading it in an audio-visual format, for retrieval and review whenever you want.

That hard drive isn't just your brain, it can include your entire body, since memories can also be stored in it from past experiences.

As previously mentioned, the questions are *implied.* For example, the first implied question is, "What is your goal, the thing you most want to do or become?" The second implied question is, "What are some of the positive things about your childhood that you remember?", and so on.

The process itself will help remind you of things you may have forgotten, and put you in touch with various aspects of yourself, your life and experiences. You may like and/or have more to say about some things more than others. But more important than liking or disliking something, is stating things *as they are*, as they occur to you, without self-censorship. Another part of the process will allow you to prioritize what you will focus on and utilize.

To gain the maximum benefit, give as much information as you can. You will be able to review it later.

To prepare for the Interview, keep the questions open on the device you're using to do the recording, if possible, or on another one close at hand. A laptop or other computer with a camera would be ideal, though you may be able to do the process successfully with a phone.

First, read the question silently to yourself. When you're ready to begin to record your answer, start recording on your device. Stop recording at the end of *each* answer. Proceed this way through all the questions. You will create a narrative comprised of answers to a series of questions about yourself.

# Future Self: Becoming Who You Want to Be

The first question establishes your *future* goal. It may pertain to business, health, a relationship, a career, travel, etc. Read each question first and, when you're ready, record your answer, taking as much time as you need to provide all of the *details* that come to mind. Don't hold back, don't censor yourself, or limit the vision of what you want. And also, don't rush yourself. You can stop, or pause, recording in between questions, if you need more time to reflect on the answer.

Since this segment deals with your as yet unaccomplished goal, you can future tense terms like "I want", or "I will". For example, if your goal is to have a certain kind of business, career, etc., you can say, "My goal, is to have an internet business. I *want* to have a clean, spacious environment. I *want* it to be in a beautiful location, and I *want* to have, etc.", or if you're already more comfortable and confident at this time, you could say, "My goal, is to have an internet business. I *will* have a clean, spacious environment. It *will* be in a beautiful location, and it *will have,* etc."

Either way will work. When stating your goal, just be as detailed as possible.

1. My goal, the thing I most want to do or become is...
2. Some challenges I may face in accomplishing my goal are...
3. Some of the resources and skills I may need to succeed include...
4. Some of the people who may assist me are...
5. The qualities in me I wish to develop are...

In order to proceed towards our goal, we must know where we are starting from.

# Taking Your Inventory

The next questions give you the opportunity to give an honest assessment of important aspects of your life, things that contributed to who you are today, some of your strengths and weaknesses, personal resources, areas in need of development, etc.

1. Positive things about my childhood that I remember are...
2. The people I love, who I care about the most, are...
3. The values that I try to live by are...
4. My greatest successes up until now have been...
5. Some of the challenges I have faced were...
6. I am most proud of having accomplished...
7. Some of the talents I have are...
8. Some of the things that come easiest for me are...
9. The things that seem hardest for me to do or learn are...
10. The people who've been the most positive influences in my life were...
11. The things that they helped me with the most were...
12. The things I would've liked to have done better at are...
13. The skills and resources I would've needed are...
14. The skills I now have and can draw upon to accomplish my goal are...
15. The skills I still need to attain or develop to accomplish my goal are...
16. The people I can count on who will assist me to attain my goal are...
17. The things I am most grateful in my life for are...
18. The way I'd describe my sense of humor is...
19. Some of the things that make me laugh are...
20. Some of the things I will need to accomplish my goal are...
21. In terms of following through with my goals in general, I tend to be...

22. What motivates me to pursue my goals is...
23. When I face obstacles to accomplishing my goals I tend to...

## The Unasked Questions

1. The reason(s) I want to accomplish this...
2. Once I've accomplished my goal I will feel...

Your answers to these two questions may seem, and indeed be, simple enough. And yet they can lead you like a guiding light to even deeper realizations about who you are and what motivates you.

In fact, while your goal may remain the same, your reason(s) for wanting to achieve and accomplish it may change.

As you proceed with the process, other unasked questions may occur to you. Feel free to add them, and your responses to them, to bring out even more useful details and information, to make this a richer, fuller reference resource for you. You can add them, at any time, which is easier to do now with various available computer programs.

This process is lighting the fuse, igniting and stimulating more of your own *creativity*. So, from the very beginning, you are actively moving towards the fulfillment of your goal.

# Reviewing Your Inventory

When you're ready, take the time to watch the completed Interview section, preferably several times. In doing so, you'll have the opportunity to review, and reflect on, the content you revealed, as well as to accept, understand and appreciate yourself. Notice how it feels to see and hear yourself in this video.

You will also want to focus more on the *information* and, and what you're learning about yourself, and less on the "performance". This is about something much deeper than a video selfie, it's about who you are and who you are choosing to *become*.

Use the initial Interview video to remind yourself about all of the things you already know, have done, etc., *but* that you don't always have at the forefront of your conscious awareness. The more thorough you are, the more likely that you'll recall and provide information, details, etc., that will be valuable in other parts of the process, and in your accomplishing your goal.

# The Accomplished State

After reviewing your Interview, you are going to leap forward and describe your future goal in the *present tense.* Your first Interview question had you express your *future goal.* The next questions had you provide details about yourself, some of your past experiences, people and things that are important to you, attitudes and personal resources, etc.

Now, instead of speaking in terms of "I *want* to do, I *will* have, etc.", you'll be speaking in terms of "I *now* do, I *now* am, I *now* have, etc." This is called the Accomplished State.

By putting, and stating, the goal in the Accomplished State, in the *present* tense, this part of the process brings the actual realization of your goal closer and more within reach, it's become *clearer* and more *tangible.* You are now finding it easier to see and feel what is true for you and more easily align with it.

You'll also become aware – either while stating them, or later when you review them – of the things that you're comfortable with, and feel confident about...as well as those things that may not *now* ring true.

Both are valuable. Becoming aware of the things that *don't* ring true, or that no longer reflect your goals, thoughts and feelings, helps you to clarify what's true for you now. Should there be things you aren't comfortable with now, you can always re-do this segment, focusing on expressing those things that do ring true for you and that you want to make real.

If you encounter things seem to strongly contradict what you consciously want, then a process like Standing in Spirit can help you clarify and resolve such issues.

You'll want the Accomplished State interview to also be as rich in detail as possible. Your own innate inner wisdom, that which may lay below your conscious mind, may surprise you. So, don't be too concerned if some things that you originally felt were part of your goal don't seem to be any longer, or if other things suddenly appeared that you didn't think of, or include, in your original stated goal, or *how* you would accomplish it.

There is a question below (No.5) that allows you to address this.

Just like when you began the Interview process, and provided the information about your past up until that time, you are *looking back* at what happened, what you did, since you first began your personal quest, to accomplish your goal.

Remember, you are expressing all of the details in the *present* state, the Accomplished State:

1. The goal that I accomplished is...
2. Some of the challenges I faced and overcame to accomplish it are...
3. Some of the resources and skills I acquired include...
4. Some of the people who assisted me are...
5. What was different about actually accomplishing my goal was...
6. Having accomplished my goal makes me feel...

Once you have completed question 6., stop recording and pause for a few seconds. Then, turn your camera back on and record yourself silently staring into the camera, for at least 30 seconds, while you continue to focus on *how it felt to accomplish your goal*.

*You are now capturing...*

# The Frequency of Fulfillment

In the first Interview process, we posed the two Unasked Questions, which essentially were *why* you want to achieve and accomplish your goal and *how* you will feel when you do.

As you progressed through the Accomplished State interview, moving towards question 6., you were entering more of what's called a *peak* state, a term dating back to the 1960s, and which, while it has undergone a lot of changes in terms of research and understanding, is still commonly understood to represent a certain optimal state of mind, mood, somatic experience, etc.

In Future Self terminology, this is called the Frequency of Fulfillment. You may remember the first modality, in my original Future Self experience, that described various *frequencies* for optimal health that we would learn to *attune* ourselves to.

Here's how the **Frequency of Fulfillment** works, what it does and how to use it.

As mentioned, the Frequency of Fulfillment helps you to *entrain*, or synchronize, yourself with the frequency, state, vibration, etc., that you attained by the time you finished the Accomplished State interview.

You do this by *going face-to-face with yourself* on video, i.e. specifically watching the silent video that you recorded of yourself after completing all of your responses to the six questions in that segment. As you view it, you begin to recapture the *thoughts and feelings* you were having, even the same breath rate and facial expressions, etc. In this way, you are entraining and *recharging yourself* to this state in a very short period of time, perhaps as little as 30 seconds.

Since you have already recorded yourself in this state on video, you can use it to "tune" yourself to this state whenever you want. Your Frequency of Fulfillment, this higher vibrational state, now becomes your *baseline* state, that which you can *start* your day with and build upon. And it can be used to initiate, as well as enhance, almost any form of *meditation*.

It also becomes a *mirror* to look in that reliably reflects you in an optimal state, no matter how you feel when you first look into it. As you progress with your Future Self practice, i.e. utilizing all of the components that you created and will have access to, you can continue to create newer - and longer - Frequency of Fulfillment videos when you become aware of attaining a new peak state.

The Frequency of Fulfillment is one process that you may also feel comfortable with, and benefit from, using at other times and places throughout your day. Since it's quite common for people to be looking at their phones, in every possible location and situation, etc., you need not feel uncomfortable taking the opportunity, as previously mentioned, to recharge yourself by periodically watching this silent video.

The more we attune ourselves to, and live in, the Frequency of Fulfillment, we realize that we don't need a *reason* to be happy, fulfilled, confident, grateful, positive, etc., we choose to be and feel that way *now*, in every flowment, while we move towards our goal. The accomplishment may be delayed but the happiness, peace, joy and fulfillment needn't be.

This is a good place to clarify that you aren't working towards a dependence on this kind of technology, you are using it to attain and familiarize yourself with *how it feels* to gain this improvement and make it part of your own, ongoing *internal* process, in every moment of your life. In fact, all of the steps of the Future Self process can be synthesized as an internal, meditative process.

# Monitoring Your Progress

As is often case in life, you may find yourself at an impasse, here or there, that serves to remind you of the need to acquire, and/or develop, certain tools, or abilities, that you don't currently have. So, it's best to be self-honest, recognize rather than resist the obstacle, i.e. see it for what it is, and – quite literally – *ask yourself* what you need in order to surmount it.

You may then intuit what you need, which of course may also include, asking assistance from someone else who has a particular, necessary skill that you know you lack. There's an element of the process designed to give you the opportunity to deal with this, as you'll see.

*But first...*

# The Mindbender

You can use this technique when reviewing any/all of your videos. It can create a kind of multidimensional effect. It's easiest to do if you have a computer, or a TV, on which to watch your videos, and a separate camera to record yourself as you are watching and interacting with yourself on the screen.

For example, if you are going to review your Interview on a computer, lap top, tablet, or phone, or TV, you may first want to set up a separate camera (on a tripod, or a suitable steady surface, like a table, bookshelf, etc.). It's best to check first that the Mindbender video you will now be recording will be able to capture both your recorded Interview and as much of your face as possible.

While you want to make sure to capture and record your *responses* to your prerecorded Interview, an over-the-shoulder angle, from behind you, capturing you observing yourself on-screen can be an interesting experience to later review as well.

What you're doing here, both figuratively and literally, is creating a *closed loop*. This reinforces a core premise of the Future Self process, i.e. developing self-responsibility by establishing your accountability to, and trust in, *yourself*, not to any outside authorities, leaders, etc. This self-development is necessary in order to be able of real service, assistance, accountability and trustworthiness to others, as well as to be open to *learning* from others.

Future Self is helping to accelerate this process, to give you actual, reusable evidence and information so that you can *self-correct*.

Self-correcting requires self-honesty and by having this closed loop process, you can work through issues that may you now become more aware of, i.e. any doubts, uncertainties, defenses, etc., that you notice. Because there is no one else to confront or criticize you, etc., you may be less defensive, embarrassed, etc., than if another person was involved.

*One of the most interesting ways to use the **Mindbender** is with the…*

## The Daily Journal

The Daily Journal is an overview and recap of each day's accomplishments and progress, as well as for recognizing any obstacles that may need to be overcome. It also functions as a preparation for the next day, helping you to note the tools and resources you will need in your ongoing progress.

You will *ask yourself* these questions in the Daily Journal process. As is true for all of the questions in the Future Self process, use them as starters; you can certainly add other ones that may occur to you at any time:

1. The things that I accomplished today are…
2. The obstacles I encountered that I need to address and resolve are…
3. The tools and resources I will need to do that are…
4. Tomorrow I will accomplish…
5. The tools and resources I will need to do that are…
6. The people I might contact if I need additional help are…
7. In order to maintain and further develop my progress I will need…

# Future Self as a Mindfulness Mirror

Having spoken at the beginning of the book about mirrors, their uses and limitations, the Future Self process can be seen, and repeatedly used as, a Mindfulness Mirror. This revolutionary new goal-setting, self-awareness and consciousness expanding tool brings you face-to-face with the real expert in your own life...*you.*

The Future Self process can also bring up and help you identify various feelings, including doubts, insecurities, etc. Having a video record can help you to notice if, and where, you may have resistance to doing certain parts of the process, or to having what you say you really want, or other considerations.

So, in addition to taking a self-analytical approach, should one be working with a qualified therapist, psychoanalyst, counselor, etc., their Future Self video could be very useful in such work as well. In fact, one can participate *with* their therapist in ways not possible before.

You can use Future Self to set goals for the year and keep a library of your different successful goal completions. With Future Self you get advice, guidance and help by coming face-to-face with the person who knows, or who soon *will* know, you the best...yourself. Future Self is a great way for young people to start to focus on what they want in life, and to see themselves progressing towards, and accomplishing, it day after day, week after week, month after month, and year after year.

Future Self is a comprehensive, reusable program you can update, modify and add to as, and however, you wish.

When you embark on the journey to become your Future Self, to become who you really want to be, you are also moving forward in a process of discovering, and becoming, your own best friend.

# An Important Note

The Future Self program can open many doors to personal success, in many areas. Becoming the authority and hero in one's own life, as a fully self-responsible, self-aware and productive person is the real goal, and a core element of the spiritual teaching.

The most important step one can take, in my opinion, is to study the spiritual teaching, as presented by Billy Meier, in numerous free articles and in published books.

Some of the recommended books are:

*The Might of the Thoughts, The Way to Live, The Psyche, The Goblet of the Truth, The Decalogue,* and *The Talmud Jmmanuel.*

All can be found at:
http://www.theyfly.com/shop/products/index.html
with more to be added in the future.

# About Michael Horn

Michael Horn has consistently demonstrated enormous creativity and being well ahead of his time. Michael is the creator of the innovative, interactive, mindfulness and stress relief program, Standing In Spirit (which Michael was invited to teach to corporate and government leaders in Europe, such as **BASF, Eurochemie, Rabobank, KLM, Cyco Software, ING Bank, Meta Visie**, by a consultant to Princess Diana)

Michael's very eclectic background also includes: award-winning film director, film producer, prize-winning painter, designer/creator of the still popular fashion fad "**fingernail art**" (featured in Harper's Bazaar magazine), award-winning songwriter, one of the first creators of digital online book publishing (**ebooks/Netbooks**), inventor of the first portable, inflatable travel neck pillow, music and video producer, science researcher, national and international lecturer, university lecturer, frequent media guest, published writer, credentialed teacher, humorist, pioneer in commercial water purification applications (**Starbucks**), theatrical set designer, health care professional, creator of the **Future Self** interactive, therapeutic video technique, volunteer work with children and seniors, creator/teacher of the **Sit & Get Fit** regenerative movement videotapes and program for seniors, as well as for personnel at U.S. corporations like **Xerox** and **Candle**.

Michael has been featured in two issues of the international martial arts magazine INSIDE KUNG FU demonstrating advanced strength and flexibility Chi Gong exercises and has articles published in **Nexus, Mystic Pop** and **UFO** magazines. Additionally, he created and taught a selfdefense course for women for the **City of Los Angeles Commission on the Status of Women.**

"Breaking the Silence" is the new, award-winning, documentary about five courageous young women that Michael and his daughter produced. See more about this amazing film here.) Michael also wrote the song for the film, "I'll Be My Own Hero", which he has also personally performed at the invitation of motivational speaker, Anthony Robbins for his Fire Walk events.

As one of the first creators of ebooks, in 1995, Michael is glad to now have his own first ebook, Future Self.

Michael Horn is also the **Authorized American Media Representative** for the Billy Meier Contacts, which he has researched since 1979 (and which have now been independently proved to be absolutely, and singularly, authentic). He is the writer and producer of the new, award-winning feature length documentary, "And Did They Listen?", as well as "as the time fulfills", "The Silent Revolution of Truth", and "The Meier Contacts – The Key To Our Future Survival".

**Future Self**
From the Mind of Michael Horn

# Songs of Michael Horn

## I'll Be My Own Hero

I was looking for somebody to believe in someone who'd save the day when things go wrong
someone who'd live and die for all the things I only cry for someone who'd change my life change it with a song

I was looking for someone with all the answers someone who'd show me how to play the game and be stronger than the sadness all the anger and the madness how long can I hide the one I'm trying to find

I'll be my own hero I'll make my own magic
I'll change the endings that used to be tragic
I'll be all that I am without armor or mask
I'll be my own hero my own hero at last

Now I don't need someone to come and save me to show me how my life's supposed to be cause I keep on taking chances finding my own answers love's the only savior
I will ever need

I'll be my own hero I'll make my own magic
I'll change the endings that used to be tragic
And all through my life I'll let love lead me on
I'll be my own hero I'll sing my own song

**Dream the Dream**

Somebody said you mustn't dream and you believed that lie you carried it for oh so long till your dream said goodbye now your dream has reappeared oh can it still be true more than a dream has come alive it is the real you

Dream the dream you want to dream give it to the world what's the sense of holding back your dream your precious pearl dream the dream you want to dream and you will be surprised the dream you dream will come alive before your very eyes

You rub your eyes can you be sure oh how can it be true then a little voice inside you says "It's really up to you just pretend love never ends and you will see it's true when you believe in your own dreams your dreams believe in you"

Dream the dream you want to dream give it to the world what's the sense of holding back your dream your precious pearl dream the dream you want to dream and you will be surprised the dream you dream will come alive before your very eyes

And when you want to find your dream wherever you may be look inside your very heart for all eternity

Dream the dream you want to dream give it to the world what's the sense of holding back your dream your precious pearl dream the dream you want to dream and you will be surprised the dream you dream will come alive before your very eyes

## Sing the Song of Life

If your life has lost its meaning and you face the world alone your
dreams they all are broken your heart sinks like a stone somewhere
a voice is calling and its song will find your heart let the melody
awaken all the love locked in the dark

Sing that your heart may feel sing that your wounds may heal sing
with pure abandon sing to set things right sing from every mountain
top sing the song of life

As the song of life awakens everyone who hears its notes seek the
broken hearted who like you yearn to be whole fill your voice with
love's sweet calling that your song may find its mark let your
melody awaken all the love locked in their hearts

Sing that your heart may feel
sing that your wounds may heal sing with pure abandon sing to set
things right sing from every mountain top sing the song of life

Let the ice-cold snows of winter gently thaw at spring's return let
the sound of joyful laughter echo in the hearts that yearn to

Sing that your heart may feel sing that your wounds may heal sing
with pure abandon sing to set things right sing from every mountain
top sing the song of life

# Hope of Tomorrow

You wander through the world
you know there's something you were born to do
and everywhere you wander you hear your destiny call out to you
it's ringing true

For you are the hope of tomorrow yours are the dreams that never
sleep you you're the one for whom life has just begun you will find
the stars within your reach

You're gathering together everybody that you meet along the way
showing them the power of a heart that's free to give its love away
they'll hear you say

For you are the hope of tomorrow yours are the dreams that never
sleep you you're the one for whom life has just begun you will find
the stars within your reach

But in a darkened moment when you fear there's
not enough reason to keep going instead of giving up remember

For you are the hope of tomorrow yours are the dreams that never
sleep you you're the one for whom life has just begun you will find
the stars within your reach

**Here's to Us**

We who've searched so long and lonely for the strength to live life
boldly while the world was telling us it didn't care many times we
have been lied to been denied and even tried to end it all trapped in
a moment in a moment of despair

We who've bent beneath the pressure while we still unearthed the
treasure with our last ounce of strength left we persevered with the
wisdom born of patience and the blessings of creation we look back
upon the hurdles all the hurdles we have cleared

Here's to us resting in each other's arms here's to us taken high
above all harm here's to us and the strength to carry on every day
every way forever sweetly dawning here's to us

So we say to all the others who have recently discovered the
strength that they've been hiding through the years now there's
more than just survival take joy in your arrival in a world that lives
for love for love instead of fear

Here's to us resting in each other's arms here's to us taken high
above all harm here's to us and the strength to carry on every day
in every way forever sweetly dawning here's to us

**Brother River**

We are man and woman seeking for the way to get along with all
the trees and seas and animals before our light is gone we'll stay
here for our lifetime we'll go the way we came and the only thing
we'll leave this earth is our body and our name

Now there're mountains of aluminum where forests used to stand
and the acres of used papers try to suffocate our land we'll stay
here for our lifetime we'll go the way we came and the only thing
we'll leave this earth is our body and our name

I am one with brother river mother earth and sister air I am spirit
can you hear it my voice is everywhere

So father guide your little ones with strong but tender hands that
they may see the morning sun rise on the newborn land they'll stay
here for their lifetime they'll go the way they came and the only
thing they'll leave this earth is their body and their name

I am one with brother river mother earth and sister air I am spirit
can you hear it my voice is everywhere

## Time, Time

Come let me put my arm around your shoulder there are things
that we will learn as we grow older sometimes love can turn to pain
when we expect the same feelings from each other remember
feelings change

It takes time before our hearts will become steady in the meantime
we must love and still be ready to accept each changing mood as an
offering of food eating all that we are given if we're hungry for the
truth

Time, time and time once again we turn our bodies to the ever-
changing winds over and over it never will end we are always just
beginning to be learning to be living always just beginning to be
friends

Now cutting through the bonds of past conditions we must use the
flaming sword with great precision let the tender part remain like a
babe new born in rain free from all illusion here by love alone
sustain

Time, time and time once again we turn our bodies to the ever-
changing winds over and over it never will end we are always just
beginning to be learning to be living always just beginning to be
friends

Words & Music Michael Horn
All songs © 1970, 1984, 2012
Sounds
Eternal Music

Printed in Great
Britain
by Amazon